VOICE-OVER

ANGIE ESTES

VOICE-OVER

ANGIE ESTES

Oberlin College Press

www.oberlin.edu/~ocpress

Publication of this book was supported in part by a grant from the Ohio Arts Council.

Ohio Arts Council
A STATE AGENCY
THAT SUPPORTS PUBLIC
PROGRAMS IN THE ARTS

Library of Congress Cataloging-in-Publication Data

Estes, Angie
        Voice-Over / Angie Estes.
        (The FIELD Poetry Series v. 12)
        I. Title.   II. Series.

LC: 2001099854
ISBN: 0-932440-91-6   (pbk.)

for Kath

and for Tom-Bon and Beau

ACKNOWLEDGMENTS

Thanks to the editors of the following journals in which some of these poems first appeared:

American Literary Review: "Atrium"

The Antioch Review: "The Annunciation in an Initial R"

Chelsea: "Chapel," "Performance"

Crab Orchard Review: "Say *Merveille*"

FIELD: "*Amor Ornamenti*," "Narrative," "Rhapsody"

ForPoetry.com: "After Mozart," "*Bel Canto*," "Say *Merveille*"

Green Mountains Review: "Lilac Fugue"

Gulf Coast: "*Vedute Da Tempo*"

LIT: "Rebus"

Mid-American Review: "*Objects May Be Closer Than They Appear*," "Spectacular Bid"

The Paris Review: "Vermeer Fever," "*Trompe l'Oeil*"

Pleiades: "History," "Score"

Ploughshares: "*Roma Caput Mundi*"

Shenandoah: "Classical Order"

Slate: "Cell 7: The Mocking of Christ"

Southern Poetry Review: "Deposition"

TriQuarterly: "Entrance to an Imaginary Villa," "More," "Scripture"

"Now and Again: An Autobiography of Basket" appeared in the anthology *Queer Dog* (Cleis Press, 1997).

"The Annunciation in an Initial R" and "Now and Again: An Autobiography of Basket" appeared in *The Extraordinary Tide: New Poetry by American Women* (Columbia University Press, 2001).

"Rhapsody," "Narrative," and "*Roma Caput Mundi*" appeared in *Sad Little Breathings & Other Acts of Ventriloquism* (Publishing Online Press, 2001).

"Flying Information" was awarded the Poetry Society of America's Cecil Hemley Award.

Grateful acknowledgment is made to the Poetry Society of America for the Alice Fay Di Castagnola Award.

Admiration and thanks go to my editor, Martha Collins, and to all of my editors at Oberlin: Pamela Alexander, David Walker, and David Young. Thanks also to Reginald Shepherd, Marjorie Welish, and Bryan Narendorf. My gratitude to Peggy Lant and Clark Griffith: dear friends, enduring teachers. And much more than thanks to Kathy Fagan and Tom-Bon and Beau, whose voices are here.

CONTENTS

In mental life nothing which has once been formed can perish.... Let us try to grasp what this assumption involves by taking an analogy from another field. We will choose as an example the history of the Eternal City.... Of the buildings which once occupied this ancient area he will find nothing, or only scanty remains, for they exist no longer.... Their place is now taken by ruins, but not by ruins of themselves but of later restorations made after fires or destruction.

Sigmund Freud

To write music is to raise a ladder without a wall to lean it against.

Arthur Honegger

How can language alter. It does not it is an altar.

Gertrude Stein

Parfait Martinique: coffee mousse, rum on top, a little cream on top of that.

Wallace Stevens

HORS D'OEUVRE

Have another,
said Sister Alyssum, champion
of asylum—who's missing? Who's
listening? Give me more
than religion, *le mot*
juste, le jus d'orange. Outside
of work, outside the ordinary
tease before a meal
begins, serve me
canapés with smoked
may happen, appetizers
seated within reach, underneath
a canopy: skirt with a roof above
the ordinary *sans* mosquitos
singing scat. When you leave
the shops in Paris, each *madame* sings
avoir in the key of middle
need, which sounds so much
like *au revoir*, you step back in
for *champagne* and adores,
to hear what's missed
pronounced again in conjugated
light, as if to see again
is to have.

ENTRANCE TO AN IMAGINARY VILLA

How easily the edge
of this world becomes
the edge of the next,
the way the bedroom wall
of the Villa Fanius
at Boscoreale is a painting
of the entrance
to a villa whose third
and fourth stories hang
in verdigris air, impossible
to reach from here.
                    Is there a room
to let, a letter
waiting, a bird who slits
the air? It could be the home
of memory, no place,
the room where Augustine
finally found God, and it hangs
in the shade with nothing
but room to grow, room
for error, which lives there as light
lives on in the cathedral
of Chartres at night. *Open
and close me,* Augustine prayed,
*like a vowel, like a window
with no view.*
                  But who has room
for memory with its architectural
cues: receding colonnades, aproned

stage, litany of places
all spacious and named? How close
are the cows coming home
from the field? How near
are the birds not
singing? Neither high nor low
relief can be found on the terraced
paths the cows have worn
across the hills for centuries. Flat
as literal translation, something roams
around its rising rooms, repeating
O's and making vows to slide
the window close
to closed, to hear the wind
first low then rise
like the chickadee's
song, all vowels.

SCRIPTURE

I'll tell you what is meant
on condition that it be
understood, what is lent on condition
that it be returned. Chartreuse,
first ruse of spring, liqueur
of the Carthusian monks at Grenoble,
is pale green, yellow as eggs

inside fresh hens in the markets
of Firenze each spring, pale
as the grappa from Piemonte
whose label, handwritten in red
and black ink on torn
paper reads *Dear Maria,*
I have to talk to you.

Le Corbusier's statue of Mary
in the chapel at Ronchamp
swivels to bless pilgrims inside
and out, but the effigy Ruskin found
on the tomb he climbed
in Santi Giovanni e Paolo
turned out to be only half

a Venetian doge: one hand, one
cheek, one side of the forehead
wrinkled, carved to be seen only
from below like the face
of the moon we can see

or the cameo, raised relief
of love. What is lent:

the curved throat
of the road, the deer
thrown back like the *s*
in *swan*: squirrel
flat on the asphalt, carnival
mask, its own black map
of what it means.

REBUS

As in the riddle   can you get there
    from here   *membra disjecta*
things scattered   leaves detached
    from their manuscripts   millions illuminated
      in Monterey   San Simeon   Pismo
           Morro Bay   migratory   wintering

sewn onto trees   with   thin
    black thread   hanging orient
pale and peach   place   east
    of pearl   and west of
      lustre   located   adjusting
        the way

                    Abbot Suger
in twelfth-century   France
    arranged   topaz   jasper
    sapphire   onyx   on the altar
     of the Abbey of St. Denis   placed
gold and silver   chalices
      to catch   divine light
    like a line drive to first
thrown straight back   to home plate

      By things
he said   *you shall see*   *the light*
   and the light   *shall make you*   *see*

polished cherrywood screen   abalone
        inlay   behind it   licorice whip
                waves undressing
while the light looks in
                                staining
        the window

autumn's empty   silk purse
        with its hard black seam
                hymnal parted   and lips
        just opening   to sing   ribbon
that marks   the place we intend
                to return to

or remain   cathedral
        of scented mist   after rain
                                ascending   silent
castanets in the eucalyptus   steeling
        the air   with their green
                stings of breath

Lilac Fugue

The tenth century invented a way
to depict the pitch of notes
by placing them vertically
on the page the way winter hangs
its zigzag ice and April's finches perch
and sing on every limb
like notes. Rilke believed
that repeated notes rising
from the organ for centuries
inside Notre Dame
had rounded the curves
of every arch—that there are strains
of music, musical sprains, contusions
and even a bruise or two in March
whenever lilac booms.
                                        In that case,
What is the question? Stein asked
before dying after no one
responded to *What*
is the answer? Perhaps she was thinking
of phantom pain—how it remains
when the hand is gone but its home
in the brain is not—of the medieval
monks who drew elaborate bars
in illuminated books to fill
the space that remained on each line
when the text had come
to an end.
                        What winds up
the trunks of trees until there's nothing

but stars in sight? Wisteria, minding
all the way, mute
as the stars' insistence. And what
does the beech tree inscribe
on the sky with its flourish of copper
serifs? Each angle
of the conductor's baton
still holding its place
in air, the late evening sky
still lighted by its white
crossed scars of flight.

Now and Again:
An Autobiography of Basket

for Gertrude Stein

Comets are like scythes, they do not hold
your coat, although they may look
as if they are going to, just rounding
the corner into the century, but perhaps she was
speaking of commas, celestial bodies trailing
bright hair every seventy some years,
once through a lifetime if you're lucky
you see them, two women and a poodle
curved into hummocks, asleep
and slung between sheets, still now
and again her mouth would open,
grin, and then bear down
on something it looked like dahlias
she carried in her teeth and time
and time again it was my name,
so sometimes we danced, my paws
on her shoulders in the garden of Bilignin
while she sang *I am I because my little dog*
knows me to the tune of "On the Trail
of the Lonesome Pine," *each part needing its own*
place to make its own balancing
as in a sentence she said, there is a mirror
of that and another photo, too,
where we sit as we were told to
on the sofa in front of the portrait
she painted me on the wall behind, when time
and time again she told me to sit
because she loves me in that painting

she says there I am God's dog, ASCOB,
who barks all the time but is impossible
to hear, that *my* epitaph, too, should declare
Any Solid Color Other than Black
when the time comes to call
everything back to where it belongs,
to its place in some long sentence
where I was going to say we are
the commas, tipped like hammocks
in the wind, but then again now
I think, rather, we are the hammocks
in which the commas swing.

RHAPSODY

No one says it
anymore, *my darling,*
not to the green leaves
in March, not to the stars
backing up each night, certainly
not in the nest
of rapture, who
in the beginning was
an owl, rustling
just after silence, whose
very presence drew
a mob of birds—flickers,
finches, chickadees, five cardinals
to a tree—the way a word
excites its meanings. *Who*
cooks for you, it calls, *Who looks*
for you? Sheaf of feathers, chief
of bone, the owl stands
upon the branch, but does he
understand it, think *my revel,*
my banquet, my tumult,
delight? The Irish have a word
for what can't be
replaced: *mavourneen, my*
darling, second cousin once
removed of memory, *what is not*
forgotten, as truth was
defined by the Greeks.
It's the names

on the stones in the cemetery
that ring out like rungs
on a ladder or the past
tense of bells: Nathaniel Joy,
Elizabeth Joy, Amos
Joy and Wilder Joy,
and it all comes down
to the conclusion
of the cardinal: *pretty, pretty, pretty*
pretty—but pretty what?
In her strip search
of scripture, St. Teresa
was seized, *my darling*, rapt
amid the chatter
and flutter of well-coifed
words, the owl
in the shagbark hickory,
and all the attending dangers
like physicians
of the heard.

CLASSICAL ORDER

sheep horns curled at the head, limestone
head of Dionysus, acanthus leaves
finishing their upward crawl, licking
their tongues, beginning to curl—
violin scroll in high relief, wig rolled
just to the ear   *whether there be tongues,*

they shall cease   antique
silent to the eye
without taper and flute, wick
to what light, narrowed but not
diminished, perhaps diminished
but arriving at an end
and, thus, without perspective

high-pitched instrument, reedless
mouthpiece at the end, long
parallel grooves incised
on the shaft of the column—
pleated ruffle, tutu

but placed on earth, touching base
with a dewclaw,
something vestigial we carry
with us, reaching only
the dewy surface of the ground

something to turn on, then,
capital: Corinthian   column: spinal
and never plumb
with anything, segmented
stack of sobriquets,

vertebrae, from *vertere*, to turn
something to turn on
hereafter nicknamed Veronica
verus iconicus
whose handkerchief
preserves the true image

of a face, cape
passed slowly before
a charging bull
while the matador stands
immobile   *though I speak*

with the tongues
of men and of angels   consider
the pilasters that assist at the mouths
of mausoleums, think
of all the motel rooms across America
that do not want
to be disturbed

MUSIQUE D'AMEUBLEMENT

after Satie

He said it would fill up
The silence that sometimes
Descends on guests as they sip
Sherry on the sofa, just before dinner
Begins, that the sound of furniture
Being moved would be enough
To furnish those rooms
We wait in, just as the sound
Of lovers making furniture
Move in the adjoining suite
Is sometimes enough
To fill our room too.

SAY MERVEILLE

for Josephine Baker

and where lime green meets
gun barrel blue *c'est*
        horizon, thunder, evening waist
where bananas orbit mahogany
        hips—no, madrone, peeling
bark like the moon in a phase
        or the phrase we search for
to light it: *je voudrais,*
        chérie, honeysuckle
cobbled with vibrating
        blossoms—or were they
bees? Discord at the end
        of May, dismay *sans*
la chaleur de nôtre amour
        nôtre dame, la mer, ma
mère, nightmare, je voudrais
        a ray, disarray, display,
d'accord? Dis aster, dark
        star, *je voudrais retrouver*
diamond sequins
        on your lips: fireflies'
brief blossoms, constellation
        seen only at night

VERMEER FEVER

*Scientists for the first time have used a natural chemical
to dramatically increase the life spans of human cells in
laboratory dishes and perhaps make them immortal.*

The Washington Post, *January 14, 1998*

We all came down with it
in the seventeenth century, back

when it was still possible
to die. It was necessary then

to dwell on drops of rain
until all the world

wore beads, as when Vermeer, for instance,
made entire landscapes inlaid

with pearl, brass chandeliers
beaded, brick houses mortared

with pearl—and not just the necks
of women, either, but seedpearled boats,

bridges, cold silver pitchers, rivers
and ribbons and bread; of course

in some paintings, even pearls
and paintings, too, eventually came down

with Vermeer fever—beyond our reach
to cure, the way the shape

of light resembling a pearl
could be conjugated

into *passé composé* and finally
turn into light. We were like

the squirrel, high on a branch
in winter, who curves his tail forward

to cover his body and become
the initial that stands

for his name; we, too, were diagnosed,
admitted: *Je me ressemble,*

I resemble no one
so much as myself.

So many tapestries lifted,
pulled back; on every wall

a map. So many paintings
covered with glass

to ward off the fingers
of unbelievers. She has no place

among us now, that woman
Vermeer once drew in fever,

eye and earring inviting us in.
She will go on turning toward us,

                    turning away—
the way the black and white

                    of water and ice swirl around
each other in a January stream—

                    but like lilacs that no longer
bloom without the hold

                    of winter, we have no need
of necklaces, glances,

                    or desire. Full moon turning back
to a darkened place, she can keep

                    the prognosis that love
must always have.

Amor Ornamenti

It is easier to love beautiful
creatures, sweet scents, and lovely
sounds than to love
God, the eighth-century scholar
Alcuin said, so God invented
passementerie, ornamental
trimming for curtains, pillows,
and gowns—gold braid, silver
beads, the silk-and-gilt
tinsel of passion, translated
from the Greek *pathos* from Latin
passus: *suffering, to suffer*—
never passé, never out of
fashion. Howling human, winged
monster, lion-headed
body projecting from a gutter
to carry rainwater clear
of the wall: gargoyle—
as in *guttur, gargoul*, as in
gutter, in throat—narrow stony
astonished passage—liaison
to what? And where is syntax,
sentence, *my liege*, which leads to
sacrilege, the stealing
of sacred things? The presentation
and movement of the cape to
attract, receive
and direct the charge of
the bull is called

pase. The Indian name for
the buckeye tree: *hetuck,*
"eye of the buck," for the glossy
brown orbs that split
their green lids like seams.

NARRATIVE

The colonnades on St. Peter's Square
embraced Bernini's ellipse and many stories
beneath me was Rome, its own
roman à clef, home of
the Pantheon of Marcus Agrippa, built
under the Pantheon of Hadrian
where Raphael was later
buried: shell of a turtle, no place
with entrance and light
placed at the center
of its coffered dome: *
little star, asterisk, unattested
existence not established by documentary
evidence, but reliably inferred
*see *hole* *see *light*
*see *shape* of the space made
by music, a room
we can hear: pierced ceiling
that will miss the dark, which was
so clear and clever.

SAN MARCO SUITE

after Fra Angelico

Cell 3: The Annunciation

Not a gavotte, not moderately
quick in 4/4 time, and far
from the Alps where rocks
garrote the river, but a dance
nonetheless: the granite
salmon's spawn in a shallow
creek, vaulted stone
overhead where fins
flip dark to light. Drained
from Mary's coral
to Gabriel's pomegranate
gown, color is on his
side, weighted and draped
the way news approaches
but waits: a line read right
to left, the meaning undone,
unsaid like a noose
untried, all slide and knuckle
without throat.

Cell 7: The Mocking of Christ

The pages of the book have turned
to stone and cracked, but Saint Dominic,
seated on the floor to the right, reads on
while Mary sits alone
on the left, *bella cosa*
beatified—not to be confused
with *bellicose*, inclined to start
quarrels or wars, like the bodiless hands
of the Roman soldiers, positioned
around the face of Christ.
                              Kosmos,
the Greeks would call it, everything
in order like a chess game
before it begins, but *no architecture*
can be truly noble which is not
imperfect, Ruskin advised,
because it does not resemble
life—Venetian palazzos, gladioli—
one third in full bloom, one third
spent, and one third on
the way. Blindfolded
                              above and behind
Mary and the Saint, Christ
is the apex of their triangle, check
of their mate, point
toward which everything
retreats—even the gaze
of Mary, although for now
it is turned away while she
touches her cheek to make
sure she is real.

Cell 6: Transfiguration

Enter: a tenor, tense
with territory, transitive and thus
needing an object: *This necklace*
of saints suits me
to a T. Not an illustration
of a text but the text
itself a note
to sing: *I, as in iota, as in*
not one—light as the fireflies'
lightning each night—I
will be done
to the N's of the earth: noon,
north, noun, note, number, even
in November. Erratum
on the headstone:

                              -er

When time at last his days shall numb

Red light green light:
Peter, James, and John run
forward then freeze, robins
coming up the path.

SPECTACULAR BID

At post time in May, thoroughbreds and jockeys
latch themselves inside the gate and, when
the time is right, unfurl their legs in staccato
leaps into what lies ahead. Beyond
the track, ferns curled in fists unroll

themselves into the world the way di Paolo's
God wheels onto the stage the world he's made,
running over the heels of Adam and Eve
with his shopping cart full of life. Above
their heads, leaf buds heave: ripe birds breaking

into wing. Part of that wheel, with its spokes
of stone, holds up the nave at Chartres; those flying
arcs throw down and out what only wants
to go up. Believers once aspired to unprecedented
heights: they vaulted Notre Dame, Chartres,

Reims, Amiens—until at Beauvais, which would
rival them all, the walls of the choir collapsed.
As if divinely ordained that the reach should always
exceed the grasp, construction spanned centuries,
yet—though they last—no gothic cathedral's complete.

The odds are always good when favorites
compete, but wherever breath has ascended
through air, names still race in the nave: *Thunder
Gulch, Silver Charm, Proud Appeal,*
and *Demons Begone; Spectacular Bid* and *Private*

Terms, *Phantom on Tour* and *Holy Bull*;
next, *Life's Magic*, *Unbridled's Song*, then *Deeds
Not Words*, who came in last. In this photo,
Proud Appeal—or is it *Spectacular Bid?*—
does not yet know whether he will show

or place or win. Suspended in some region
between heaven and earth, horse and jockey
lean into homestretch, twin arcs flying
above the track: with only one hoof touching dirt, they
tilt toward some finish they can only imagine.

DEPOSITION

How to testify, with the ground, too,
become a figure. Not simply absence
but a kind of negative space. Brunelleschi's dome
rising over Florence; high-instepped
gray foot of the sky—what do we call
two things that belong together but exclude
each other? And when they fall asleep
like spoons, do we name them *concave*
or *convex*? It's the same as the problem with never
saying *never*: by the time you've said it,
you've already said it twice. Del Valle's dead
must have said it at least once while changing
their clothes for Judgment Day. After crossing
the river, they found their pantlegs filled—
where the holes for their legs, like witnesses,
used to be—so could never
figure out how *the dead shall put on
immortality*. Wanting to slip
into something more comfortable, they remember
their parents, recall being warned
never to write *xmas* and cross the Christ
out of Christmas, never to cross
anything joined to another: *careless*
    crisscross   wisecrack   eventide   forget
pantlegs   nighttime   nobody   deadline
    forever   behold   No longer
any question of guilt, but *Do you find the defendant
or not?* Define
your terms. The stiff cornhusks

thrust up from the hard-kerneled corn in autumn
are semaphores for what? What we see
in Giotto's painting are angels foreshortened
in anguish, wings and arms wrenched back,
not the torn holes in the sky
hovering over the body of Christ.

ATRIUM

Boscotrecase, 11 B.C.

It was an uncomfortable room, blackened
by smoke, frightful, atrocious,
blackened by fire before smoke
from the hearth escaped through a hole
in the roof. But if you dropped
the final *h*, smoke from a fire could
escape from the heart through the hole
in *focus*, coming into view
like the wind when a suspension bridge
begins its fibrillation—shaken out
like a sheet. From that bridge, the view
is long and final like the sound
of certain vowels, frankly and openly
acknowledged, confessed. What paintings hang
on the walls of the heart? A tiny landscape
flattened on black, Andromeda chained
to a rock with Perseus forever
gliding in, parakeets
posted at the corner of every
roof, none of them
in sight.

ROMA CAPUT MUNDI

Their place is now taken
by ruins, but not by ruins
of themselves but of later
restorations, Freud said
of the Senate and People of
Rome—otherwise known
as *SPQR*, inscribed
above the arch of Septimius Severus:
Senatus Populus Que Romanus
Silk Pajamas Quietly Rule Us
Seven Peaches Quite Ripe
Some Passing Qualm Resurfaced
Some Private Quarrel Revived
Same Palatial Quiz Revisited
Some Possible Quiet Remains
                              At the place
where three roads met, ancient
Romans posted news: *trivia*
they called it, for the way
that all roads lead only
to roam until we end up
at memory and find not
what we left there
but the history of how we wanted it
to be. We might as well call
the fine line finishing off
each letter of Roman type
seraph, the peonies lifting
up from the loam

and the sheaves of hosannas
we call hostas, *Romans*,
every one, rising from the
ruins of what we've become.

HISTORY

Since every work of history omits
more than it includes, one must
choose what mattered most, use
Michelangelo's art of subtraction
to take away every word
that is not the poem. Keep the gold
fleurs-de-lis and the *coeurs*
de lion, lit (as with light)
or *lit* as in lying in their French
bed of blue. Keep the statue
from Samothrace but say *adieu*
to her view, and keep August
so that goldfinches will finally
mate and there will be purple
and white thistledown to line
their nests. Since whatever color
we can see is the only color
an object's not, fill up the poem
with blue and let it try each day
like the ocean to turn itself
into what it is not. Then love
the poem as the poem
loves the color blue and end
as Italians do after
a long meal, with something bitter, *amaro*,
or searing, a *grappa*.

THE ANNUNCIATION IN AN INITIAL R

But whose initial? Left here, illuminated
      but abandoned by its text. Surely R stands
for religion, *religare*, something to bind us
      back, to remind that—whether reading, kneeling,
or waving goodbye—a word can enter
      our womb in a breath. Bordered with heads,
each open mouth tongued orange or blue
      with the tip of a pen, the letter R could be
autumn, all parchment and loss, each leaf
      embedded with flame.

More like *enunciation*, I should think,
      with the lungs a heavy butterfly heaving
its cocoon, and the conception some act
      of ventriloquism, immaculate and marooned.
Perhaps R is for rental—as in the villa
      where they sit, Mary and Gabriel tilting
their heads. And the gold leaf rolling in
      wherever space remains is nothing
but time, in which everything floats. Is this the way
      rooms imagine us to be: round-shouldered
and arched, all presence and tense, waiting
      for words to arrive in our ear? Space
now fulfilled, place where bulbs are forced
      to bloom—like skulls without thoughts, are they empty
without us? Initials can begin

or put an end to a name, tell stories,
        train vines, and use the bodies of others
to form their own shape; jungle gyms
        of intention, designed to mean
this one and not another, initials took the place
        of people, already replaced
by words, until they finally took over
        the page and made everything
in their image. Anthropomorphic, historiated, foliate:
        they became, like us, inhabited.

If *R* is for annunciation, then *T* can signal
        crucifixion: cross illuminated, tipped
on its side, cartwheeling to Golgotha,
        where *X* marks the spot. *Te igitur,* You therefore,
clementissime Pater, per Jesum Christum Filium tuum Dominum nostrum,
        supplices rogamus, ac petimus
the priest chants, arms and palms espaliered
        at his sides. Slowly lowered, the hands meet
again, cupping each other the way Adam and Eve
        hid from God their most private
parts, the parts he could not bear
        to see. Like flags waved by sailors
from decks of separate ships, their hands
        made the semaphore which means
        end of word.

SCORE

It does not say precisely
what it means, the way notes
inscribed and hung
on lines do not sound
the same as music, and the horse's
lips, nibbling *vibrato*, nudge
everything close to the center
of song, though they can't be said
to sing. In Fra Angelico's *Annunciation*,
it's more difficult to open
the lips of Gabriel than to remember
when Easter falls: *the first Sunday*
following the full moon that occurs
on or next after March 21, also known
as the beginning
of spring. For all we know,
it could be the birthday
of Thaumus, Greek god
of the sea, whose name means
wonder, unable or unwilling to say
what he means. His daughter Iris
took rainbows for wings
and rowed words like boats
to gods: *ascend, descend, get in, say it*
again, iris in, iris out. Adjustable aperture
unlike the grave.
                    What is a line
of descent but something we're
after: *Repeat*

after me: doorway, loggia, arcade,
receipt: Be my entrance, portico, integer,
note, my point
on a line, not vanishing: point
where the ballerina speaks, high C
where we break—unlike the line
where we finish, point
of what's the point, what we miss
and always want
to make, whether or not
we have one. When Iris looked down
from her arc to the stream,
her body flew by
like a trout: *Repeat*
after me: as in *what follows*
will explain. But what kind
of descent, Mary asked Gabriel, curved
toward him yet backing
away: *Iridescent*
is what the voice looks like
the moment before
it sings, the syllables arranged
in silica *intonaco* on the angel's rainbow
wing, all glitter, glamour,
and *obbligato.*

AFTER MOZART

to be sung to "Voi che sapete," Le Nozze di Figaro

Voice, okay, pet me;
okay—closer—and, oh, more.
Dinner at eight is great with me—
solo, *d'accord?*
Parochial *paroles,*
vino rococo,
a pear carefully chosen
can appease me so.
Send tuned affection,
a pendant brassiere,
a chorus of stilettos
chanting *my dear!*
Take the perfect pitch
of the alma mater of God
and aim it a moment
toward my jugular.
Research how many
fjords envy me
not just my so-called kiltie,
no, also my squeeze.
So spear an *h* or more,
send some vowels here,
pals who will train
to sense us appear;
now try voice-over—
note the nadir:
my purrs, my meek piazzas,
lie here, cozy.
So voice, okay, pet me;

okay—closer—and, oh, more.
Don't say you'll ever leave me
alone with *l'amour*,
just say you'll always date me
solo, *d'accord?*

BEL CANTO

Col pensier il mio desir
a te sempre volerà,
e fin l'ultimo mio sospir,
caro nome, tuo sarà.

Verdi, Rigoletto

The saucer magnolias are heavy lidded *col pensier*,
too many trills they've heard
each spring *il mio desir* when April sings
bel canto, while the arcades *a te sempre volerà*
of Palladio's Basilica in Vicenza keep arching
their backs over what we mean
by God—not Jack-
in-the-pulpit but jack-of-all-
trades, *caro nome*, who knows
where the sweetbrier grows *e fin l'ultimo*, how
to talk it up a trellis *mio sospir* with needle-nose
pliers *tuo sarà.*

                According to Raphael via
Castiglione, *those that are completely*
ruined il mio desir *and no longer*
visible mio sospir *may be understood*
by those that still stand fin l'ultimo
and can be seen mio sospir, but who can decipher
forsythia in March, the flagrant
graffiti *a te sempre volerà* of spring? In Giotto's
(caro nome) "Sacrifice of Joachim,"
the hand of God reaches into the painting
and flies *mio desir* in lapis lazuli, sky

                       tuo sarà

blue breath *l'ultimo sospir* taken near

the place where stones are mistaken

for sheep when they curl up

 il mio desir to sleep. Color, *caro nome,*

a te sempre volerà, will ever fly to thee, pink

as the peignoir of the woman

hooked over her balcony overlooking

the Marais in Paris singing *yes*

mio sospir *please press*

some darkness, mio desir,

in my thoughts *tuo sarà* rain

constant as the rain

                              a te sempre

volerà: collar, coloratura,

décolletage. Before the end

il mio desir there should be

finale, some ornamental finial to touch

fin l'ultimo what's not: across the field

a flock of geese *il mio desir* lifts

like the skirt of Marilyn Monroe's dress

a te sempre volerà or the sheet

we unfurl *mio sospir* while making

the bed saying *caro, come name*

some darkness.

OBJECTS MAY BE CLOSER THAN THEY APPEAR

If it's a law
that objects appear to diminish in size
as they recede into the distance
behind us, then can it be true
that time and absence make the heart
grow fonder?
　　　　In the fifteenth century, for instance,
Paolo Uccello stayed up for days, trying
new ways to draw foreshortened bodies,
armor, and lances that all point
the same way, but when his wife got up
and called him to bed, he said, *What a sweet thing
perspective is!*
　　　　At the apparent intersection
of earth and sky, there is a point
where parallel lines converge
or disappear, depending on your point
of view, which gives it much
in common, after all, with that quick seam
of water we once drove over, in southern Illinois,
that the sign called *Nameless Creek.*

VEDUTE DA TEMPO

This time of year, even birds have stars
in their eyes, traveling north
by night; one true far place holds
the dart of their gaze as we fly
over Manhattan. Of all the fires
that slowly turn below, a single lamp
beside a bed is the only star
to which we want to go, out of all
the faces in the airport crowd,
only one will do.

The wise men knew why we want
to flee—first away from, then toward—
whatever bright thing may wink
in the sky. Like lazuli buntings,
they offered up wings and found their way
to *what remained of what used*
to be—and other spent words
for *home*: is that where they were
in the north or the south, in winter
or in spring? They knew, before Lacan,

the reason we travel: *one is the image of oneself*
with which one tries, like a perpetual child,
to catch up. And if misrecognition of some other
in the mirror indeed produces a self,
where better than Venice
for *méconnaissance*: damask city
of the milk-breasted goddess, coiffure
plaited in gold, city of so many men found
in female dress, a law had to be passed

against it, courtesans forbidden to parade

in boats, courting men while clothed
in the clothing of men. Mirror held up
to its own waving image, city that could lose
the library of Petrarch and not even miss it
for a hundred years, busy posing
for another of Canaletto's views: Ca' d'Oro,
Ca' Rezzonico, reflection of St. Mark's
facade, all repeat the ancient Venetian motto,
Vedute da Tempo—reflect, refract,

and float. To begin with, nothing
of its own—but clever, adaptable, rising
on piles driven into silt, tongue
bobbing in the mouth like a boat. Now the black
beaked gondola we've hired for the night
strokes the water with its one pale wing,
cleaving canals into left and right, light
and shade, formless
then made; like antlers pushing
from the skull each May, the oar

touches something finally called *bottom,*
cuts velvet, and takes us back
the way we came. Stepping from the boat
to the stones of the street, at what point
can we say we have been
to *Venice?* The word itself
wears silk brocade—is flowing, loose,
unnavigable—but stars still bloom
across it each night, watch themselves lit
by some dark lagoon.

CHAPEL

Scabbard *sans* dagger;
sheath or hooded cape, shrine
of hanging shoots that eventually find
the ground and root, tightening
trunks around a tree they never
mention. They worship that way
for centuries until rot leaves
only architecture's gesture
of embrace, reliquary
with no trace of a relic.
                                    Who first imagined
the banyan—all gape and token—God's idea
of topiary, everything clipped in the shape
of nothing. Built in the thirteenth century,
Sainte Chapelle—its walls made of nothing
but light—was designed to hold
holy relics of the passion
of Christ: the Crown of Thorns, a piece of the True
Cross, fragments of the Holy Lance, Holy
Sponge, Christ's Mantel and Shroud, the Precious
Blood, and the Milk and Hair
of the Virgin. *One of the most beautiful residences of*
paradise, a fourteenth-century theologian called it.
                                    Flamboyant ribs,
highly elaborate, embellished, ornate—*flamboyer*, to blaze—
and why not? The light stayed on
while the relics went out, and the chapel
turned into *topos* incarnate, the body
of place. It's where we want

to be: *Like no place on earth,*
is what we say, as the rose roulette window
revolves overhead and we stumble
inside, a pair of dice.

                    Medieval saints placed all bets
on light they could hold like Bordeaux in a glass, called
it fair, made it bear the weight
of stone. They believed
the Persians when they said
hedge your bets, *pairi-daeza*, put a wall
around anything you might want
to keep. The caul and the body, apricot glaze
over *tarte aux pommes*: such a thin layer
between stone and hope, the violet nave
and air. From *someplace*,

                         maybe *the* place, saints gaze
through veined windows, like *sommeliers*, and nod
their advice: say *banyan*, say
snake eyes, say *building*, say *wall*;
say *chapel*, *c'est lips* that give shape
to whatever comes
between them, enclose
open space, make pleasure
spoken.

FLYING INFORMATION

What's between them cannot be
said, although it has been held
between black marks and quoted
the way walls hold
the place we call *temple*
long after the roof's
given way. *Gone*
is what we say, but how
to quote what once was
there: *departure,*
arrival, on time. And how
to punctuate them
in a sentence, two
at each end, upright
but bent slightly like the fingers
of Christ—hard to say
whether he is giving
a blessing or quoting
the words he just spoke:
Benedictio latina.
And also with you.
(And I quote.)
Finger puppets engaged
in liturgy, quotation marks
were separated like the two halves
of the soul Plato named, forever nodding
to each other from opposite ends
of a sentence—*and also with you*—the distance
between them the same

as between the cow in the field
and the egret following closely, always
behind, waiting
just off to the side: still, white,
and hungry. What's in between them?
Only everything that can be said,
which is to say "nothing
comes close." (And I quote.)
And also with you: to bless,
to speak well of, to say well—
"well"—or at the benediction,
well said. According to Quintilian,
an orator preparing to speak
would hold up his hand, first
and second fingers extended, thumb
resting lightly on the curved
fourth and fifth. Not waving,
exactly. *Schedule, delay,*
missed connection, despite the signals
from the catcher and coach
on third. Here's something
quotable: "the swallowtail sings
chrysanthemum, zinnia,
sweet alyssum, while the bees
hold the bass note *mums,*
mums, mums." The antennae inscribe
the hieroglyph for quotation: sky
with pelicans, flying
in formation.

TROMPE L'OEIL

Zeuxis painted grapes so real
that birds came down
to peck, but Parrhasius painted
a curtain that Zeuxis asked him to
pull back.
                    What is a curtain
but a promise that something lies
behind it, nothing
but definition, burgundy
velvet, draped. But *Why a little curtain*
of flesh on the bed of our
desire? Blake never tired of
asking, though Pliny had already
decreed that the best
painting of all would be
a painting of a curtain
since paintings should *disclose*
even what they hide.
                    Around 500 B.C.
some Greek no longer believed
everything he saw
needed to be
shown, but only the angle
from which it is seen: a back
too short from neck to
waist, backing out of
a frame, would mean
grief; head next to shoulder, cheek
on knee could say *bent* or

let's see—the stage built
in perspective

                at Teatro Olimpico
in Vicenza might be a stage
for love, streets narrowing
to a place where it looks as if
we could walk forever.

PERFORMANCE

The way fog speaks
                        above the voice
                                        of a river
or twenty Roman heads
                            along a museum wall
                                                    look back
and call
               the one body
                           among them, torso
touching down
                    lifting off
                              like a place,
I mean *plane*,
                    trying to land
                              was the way
the possum lumbered
                        toward us in the rain,
                                          twelve *something*
hanging on her, little bolts
                    of fur,
                            full-length chinchilla coat
knotted
            and molting.
                          She was an aria
in lilac fume,
                  heart-shaped, of course,
                                and beating
beneath a dress, lace
                leaping
                      stage left
at the breast.

Recitative: *Whose cello first opened the air?*
Chorus: *The beech trees are wild*

with apostrophes.

(Remember the gravestone engraved "Little Eddie,"
   an eight-inch, curled, sleeping white lamb; the sugar maples
       dropped their chartreuse lace hankies.)

They say it's not realistic—

impossible, even—

to sing

an aria while dying,

and perhaps that's why

we love

those scenes best:

the last gasps,

the highest

last and last,

those mostly unreachable notes

almost grasped

in the thin, last tightest breaths—

how while lying

motionless

we are moved

the most—

Is it sadness

or the relief of silence

before a curtain

falls,

rising again

perhaps

to applause.

MORE

arch than sky, more vault
than heaven, roof
of the mouth, more tent
than motet covering the space between
notes. *Hautbois, hautboy,*
high wood, oh boy—is that the tune
the oboe hums? Above
the nave, triforium, clerestory,
vault, every arch points
to what? Architecture
is the building
of interior space: a cathedral, a glove
for the hand of God, gladiolus,
foxglove ascending as if
there's no end. What then? Music
is what is left of lustre, heading
west: the shape of what's spread
between the ceiling's
ribs, vaulted beaks
of how many birds in the nest
asking for

NOTES

I assured you, however, that I would say nothing new,
nothing that was really mine, and yet nothing that was
basically borrowed, for from whatever source we learn
anything it is ours unless by chance forgetfulness takes
it from us.

Francesco Petrarca
Rerum familiarium libri
translated by A. S. Bernardo

"Entrance to an Imaginary Villa"

Villa of P. Fannius Synistor at Boscoreale, fresco, 40-30 B.C., The
Metropolitan Museum of Art.

Saint Augustine, *Confessions*, translated by Henry Chadwick
(1991).

Frances Yates, *The Art of Memory* (1966).

"Scripture"

John Ruskin, *The Stones of Venice* (1853).

Rudolf Arnheim, "Sculpture: The Nature of a Medium," *To*
the Rescue of Art (1992).

"Rebus"

Abbot Suger, *Abbot Suger on the Abbey Church of St. Denis and its*
Art Treasures, edited, translated, and annotated by Erwin
Panofsky (1979).

Otto Von Simson, *The Gothic Cathedral: Origins of Gothic Archi-*
tecture & the Medieval Concept of Order (1989).

"Lilac Fugue"

Rainer Maria Rilke, Letter to Mary and Antoinette Windisch-
graetz, 1924. Quoted in William H. Gass, *Reading Rilke:*
Reflections on the Problems of Translation (1999).

Umberto Eco, *Art and Beauty in the Middle Ages* (1986).

"Now and Again: An Autobiography of Basket"
Gertrude Stein, "Poetry and Grammar," *Narration* (1935), and *The Autobiography of Alice B. Toklas* (1936). "The Trail of the Lonesome Pine" (Barrad Macdonald and Harry Carroll) was Stein's favorite song.
Photograph of Stein and her dog Basket: *Gertrude Stein, Paris, 1946*, by Horst.
ASCOB is an official American Kennel Club designation.
Renate Stendhal, *Gertrude Stein in Words and Pictures* (1994).

"Rhapsody"
Oak Grove Cemetery, Delaware, Ohio.

"Classical Order"
1 Corinthians 13.

"Say *Merveille*"
Je voudrais, by Salvet, Ithier, Coquatrix, from *Paris mes amours* (1959).
Virginia Woolf, *The Waves* (1931).

"Vermeer Fever"
Edward Snow, *A Study of Vermeer* (1994).
Lawrence Gowing, *Vermeer* (1970).

"*Amor Ornamenti*"
Umberto Eco, *Art and Beauty in the Middle Ages* (1986).

"Narrative"
Leonard Barkan, *Unearthing the Past: Archaeology and Aesthetics in the Making of Renaissance Culture* (1999).

"San Marco Suite"
William Hood, *Fra Angelico at San Marco* (1993).
John Ruskin, *The Stones of Venice* (1853).
Oak Grove Cemetery, Delaware, Ohio.

"Spectacular Bid"
Giovanni di Paolo, *The Creation and the Expulsion of Adam and Eve from Paradise*, The Metropolitan Museum of Art.

"Deposition"

Hernán Castellano-Girón, watercolor and ink (1988), after *"Sala de espera," de La vision comunicable*, by Rosamel del Valle (1956).

Giotto, *Deposition of Christ*, Scrovegni Chapel, Padua.

Rudolf Arnheim, "Negative Space in Architecture," *To the Rescue of Art* (1992).

1 Corinthians 15:52-53.

"Atrium"

The Imperial Villa at Boscotrecase (frescoes), The Metropolitan Museum of Art.

Maxwell L. Anderson, *Pompeian Frescoes in the Metropolitan Museum of Art* (1987).

"Roma Caput Mundi"

Sigmund Freud, *Civilization and Its Discontents*, translated by James Strachey (1961).

"History"

Michelangelo: "By sculpture, I understand an art that takes away superfluous material; by painting, one that attains its result by laying on." Quoted in Mary McCarthy, *The Stones of Florence* (1963).

Michelangelo, "Letter to Messer Benedetto Varchi," from Rome, March 1547, in *Michelangelo: Life, Letters, and Poetry*, edited by George Bull (1987).

"The Annunciation in an Initial R"

Don Silvestro dei Gherarducci, *The Annunciation in an Initial R*, tempera and gold leaf on parchment, The British Library.

Otto Pächt, *Book Illumination in the Middle Ages* (1986).

"Score"

Fra Angelico, *Annunciation*, San Marco, Florence, north dormitory.

William Hood, *Fra Angelico at San Marco* (1993).

Nikolaus Harnoncourt, *The Musical Dialogue*, 1984.

"Bel Canto"
Epigraph: "In my thoughts, my desire/will always fly to you,/ and at the end my last breath,/beloved name, will be you."
Leonard Barkan, *Unearthing the Past: Archaeology and Aesthetics in the Making of Renaissance Culture* (1999).

"Objects May Be Closer Than They Appear"
Giorgio Vasari, *The Lives of the Artists*, translated by George Bull (1965).

"Vedute Da Tempo"
Mary McCarthy, *Venice Observed* (1963).
Perry Meisel, "The Unanalyzable." Rev. of *Jacques Lacan*, by Elizabeth Roudinesco. *New York Times Book Review*, April 13, 1997.

"Chapel"
Michel Dillange, *The Sainte Chapelle*, translated by Angela Moyon (1994).
Hans Jantzen, *High Gothic: The Classic Cathedrals of Chartres, Reims, Amiens* (1984).
Otto Von Simson, *The Gothic Cathedral: Origins of Gothic Architecture & the Medieval Concept of Order* (1989).

"Flying Information"
Moshe Barasch, *Giotto and the Language of Gesture* (1987).

"Trompe l'Oeil"
Leonard Barkan, *Unearthing the Past: Archaeology and Aesthetics in the Making of Renaissance Culture* (1999).
E. H. Gombrich, *The Story of Art* (1995).
William Blake, "The Book of Thel" (1789).

"Performance"
Oak Grove Cemetery, Delaware, Ohio.

"More"
John Ruskin, *The Stones of Venice* (1853).
This poem is for Tom-Bon.

About the Author

Angie Estes is also the author of *The Uses of Passion*, winner of the Peregrine Smith Poetry Prize. She is currently a visiting professor at The Ohio State University.

A Note on the Type

The text of this book was set in Bembo. Bembo was modeled on typefaces cut by Francesco Griffo for Aldus Manutius' printing of *De Aetna* in 1495 in Venice, a book by the Renaissance writer and humanist scholar Pietro Bembo about his visit to Mount Etna. Griffo's design is considered one of the first of the old style typefaces that were used as staple text types in Europe for 200 years. The italic is modeled on the handwriting of the Renaissance scribe Giovanni Tagliente.

The design fonts were set in Charlemagne. During the reign of the Emperor Charlemagne in the eighth and ninth centuries, the use of classical roman letterforms was revived. These letterforms were the basis of the highly refined versal capitals of late tenth-century England, which were the inspiration for Carol Twombly's 1989 Adobe Originals typeface.